THE
RECONSTRUCTION ERA

RAGE COMPOSITION
OME COMMON FOODS
Food
Breakfast
Wheatgerm
Potatoes
Beefsteak
Bread
Butter
Milk
Dinner
Blue fish
otatoes
Beets
Butter
Rice
Supper
Cornmeal

ICAN–AMERICAN HISTORY

THE RECONSTRUCTION ERA

by BETTYE STROUD with VIRGINIA SCHOMP

mc Marshall Cavendish
Benchmark
New York

ACKNOWLEDGMENTS

The authors and publisher are grateful to Jill Watts, professor of history
at California State University, San Marcos, for her perceptive comments on the manuscript,
and to the late Richard Newman, civil rights advocate, author, and senior research officer
at the W. E. B. DuBois Institute at Harvard University,
for his excellent work in formulating the series.

∞

EDITOR: JOYCE STANTON   EDITORIAL DIRECTOR: MICHELLE BISSON
ART DIRECTOR: ANAHID HAMPARIAN   SERIES DESIGNER: MICHAEL NELSON

MARSHALL CAVENDISH BENCHMARK 99 WHITE PLAINS ROAD TARRYTOWN, NEW YORK 10591-9001
www.marshallcavendish.us Text copyright © 2007 by Bettye Stroud All rights reserved. No part of this book may be reproduced or uti-
lized in any form or by any means electronic or mechanical including photocopying, recording, or by any information storage and retrieval
system, without permission from the copyright holders. All Internet sites were available and accurate when this book was sent to press.
LIBRARY OF CONGRESS CATALOGING-IN-PUBLICATION DATA: Stroud, Bettye, 1938- The Reconstruction era / by Bettye M. Stroud with
Virginia Schomp. p. cm. — (Drama of African-American history) Summary: "Traces the history of Reconstruction, from the end of the
Civil War in 1865 to 1877, when federal troops were removed from the South"—Provided by publisher. Includes bibliographical references
and index. ISBN-13: 978-0-7614-2181-8 ISBN-10: 0-7614-2181-5 1. African Americans—History—1863-1877—Juvenile literature. 2.
Reconstruction (U.S. history, 1865-1877)—Juvenile literature. 3. African Americans—Civil rights—Southern States—History—19th
century—Juvenile literature. 4. African Americans—Southern States—Social conditions—19th century—Juvenile literature. I. Schomp,
Virginia. II. Title. III. Series. E185.2.S87 2007 973.8—dc22 2006012149

Images provided by Rose Corbett Gordon, Art Editor, Mystic, CT, from the following sources: Cover: Corbis Back cover: The New York
Historical Society/Bridgeman Art Library Pages i, vi, 20, 36, 48, 59, 65: The Art Archive/Culver Pictures; pages ii - iii, 8, 10, 12, 14, 27,
33, 37, 61: Corbis; pages viii, 3, 5, 24, 18, 26, 42, 46: Hulton Archive/Getty Images; page x: Stock Montage/Getty Images; pages 2, 4,
17, 28, 30, 34, 39, 50, 53, 56, 63: North Wind Picture Archives; page 22: Medford Historical Society Collection/Corbis; page 35: Time
& Life Pictures/Getty Images; page 44: The Art Archive/National Archives Washington DC.

───── A NOTE ON LANGUAGE ─────

In order to preserve the character and historical accuracy of the quoted material appearing in this book, we
have not corrected or modernized spellings, capitalization, punctuation, or grammar. We have retained the
"dialect spelling" that was sometimes used by white writers in an attempt to reproduce the way some
former slaves spoke. You will occasionally come across outdated words such as *colored* and *Negro*, which were
commonly used by both white Americans and African Americans in Reconstruction times.

Printed in China
1 3 5 6 4 2

Front cover: African-American delegates to a convention in Nashville, Tennessee, debate ways to combat injustice
during Reconstruction.
Back cover: Field hands pick cotton under the watchful eyes of a white overseer.
Half-title page: A Reconstruction-era cartoon pictures a Northern African American and his "country cousin" down South.
Title page: Students take a class in nutrition at the Hampton Normal and Agricultural Institute in Virginia, one of
the nation's first black colleges.
page vi: A black family escapes from slavery in North Carolina near the end of the Civil War.

CONTENTS

INTRODUCTION

The Reconstruction Era is the fifth book in the series Drama of African-American History. Earlier books in this series have traced the journey of African Americans from colonial times through the Civil War. Now we will explore one of the most turbulent periods in American history, Reconstruction.

The term *Reconstruction* refers to the period from the end of the Civil War in 1865 to the withdrawal of the last Union troops from the South in 1877. At the start of the war, eleven Southern states had seceded from the Union and formed the Confederate States of America. For four long years, the Confederates had fought to preserve a way of life based on slavery. The North went to war to restore the Union. Gradually, however, Northerners adopted the destruction of slavery as a second and more noble war goal.

The Civil War ended in April 1865 with the surrender of the Confederate army. Now the nation faced new and difficult questions. How should the Confederate states be reorganized and readmitted to the "reconstructed" Union? Who should decide the terms of Reconstruction, the president or Congress? And what role would four million freed slaves take in Southern society?

The process of Reconstruction was complicated by the scars of war. Four years of fighting had blazed a broad path of destruction through the conquered South. Great cities had been burned to ashes, and vast plantations lay blackened and bare. Countless refugees jammed the roads, homeless and starving. The Confederate governments had collapsed, and outlaws roamed the countryside, looting at will. The only remaining source of authority was the victorious Union army. Long after the fighting ended, hundreds of thousands of Union soldiers remained in the South to restore order and punish criminals in military courts. At the same time, federal and private agencies struggled to provide aid to the refugees and govern relations between former slaves and their former masters.

The war had also left behind a legacy of anger and distrust between the North and South. Many Northerners remained hostile toward the defeated Confederate states. In their view Southerners were traitors who deserved to be punished for seceding from the Union and bringing on the devastating war. Even Northerners who felt sympathy for their fallen enemies had widely differing ideas on how the federal government should punish former Confederate leaders, aid the freed slaves, and rebuild the South.

Meanwhile, most white Southerners felt bitter and humiliated. Many had sacrificed everything for what they saw as the "glorious cause" of Southern independence. To people who had lost sons, husbands, homes, and property, the presence of the

Former slaves gather outside a small wooden schoolhouse in Savannah, Georgia.

occupying army was almost too much to bear. One angry innkeeper in North Carolina told a journalist that the Northerners had killed his sons, burned his house, and "stolen" his slaves. All he had left was "one inestimable [valuable] privilege—to hate 'em. I git up at half-past four in the morning, and sit up till twelve at night, to hate 'em."

White Southerners also found another target for their anger: the freed slaves. Former slave owners could not accept the idea that men, women, and children who had once been their "property" were now free. They did not believe that blacks were entitled to the same rights as whites. They were determined to establish a system in which they would regain control over the former slaves.

For their part, African Americans greeted the end of the Civil War with a mixture of joy, hope, and worry. Slavery's chains were broken at last. However, tremendous obstacles stood in the path of millions of former slaves who had been given little more than their freedom. During Reconstruction, the freedpeople would struggle to find jobs, build homes, gain an education, and secure their civil rights. Their efforts would change not only their lives but the very fabric of American government and society.

Senator Charles Sumner was one of the leaders of the Radical Republicans, a congressional group that fought for the rights of the freed-people.

Chapter 1

WARTIME REHEARSALS FOR RECONSTRUCTION

AMERICANS BEGAN DISCUSSING THE CENTRAL ISSUES of Reconstruction long before the Civil War ended. As Union forces invaded the South and took over Confederate territories, the federal government had to decide how to govern the occupied lands. Congressional leaders debated several different plans for replacing the Confederate state governments with new governments loyal to the Union. Meanwhile, the president appointed temporary military governors to the occupied states and mulled over his own ideas for Reconstruction.

Another major wartime debate concerned the four million African Americans held as slaves in the South. From the moment Union troops entered Southern territories, slaves had begun to run for freedom. By the end of 1861, thousands had escaped the plantations and taken refuge behind Union lines. Gradually, the war to restore the Union had been transformed

A former slave works as an oyster peddler in Baltimore, Maryland.

into a crusade against slavery. In January 1863 President Lincoln issued the Emancipation Proclamation. That historic document did not completely end slavery. It freed only slaves held in areas in rebellion against the Union, leaving in bondage those who were held by loyal slaveholders. Still, it was a giant step toward abolition.

Emancipation led to heated debates over the fate of the former slaves. While government leaders considered different plans for defining and protecting the rights of the freedpeople, African Americans had their own ideas about freedom. For many former slaves, true freedom meant establishing their economic independence and reuniting families that had been divided under slavery. The freedpeople also would demand equal civil and political rights in the reconstructed South. "The people . . . want a reconstruction such as will protect loyal men, black and white, in their persons and property," declared African-American abolitionist leader Frederick Douglass. "The South must be opened to the light of law and liberty."

LINCOLN VERSUS THE RADICALS

President Lincoln wanted to heal the wounds of war and restore the Union as quickly and easily as possible. In December 1863 he presented a generous Reconstruction plan that he hoped would encourage the Confederate states to end their rebellion. Lincoln's Proclamation of Amnesty and Reconstruction offered a full pardon, or amnesty, to former Confederates who took an oath of loyalty to the Union and pledged to accept the abolition of slavery. The only people excluded from the amnesty were high-ranking Confederate government officials and military officers. After 10 percent of the voters in a state took the loyalty oath, they could form a new state government.

Many Northerners thought that Lincoln's "Ten Percent Plan" was *too* generous. The most outspoken critics were the Radical Republicans. This group of congressional Republicans was led by dedicated abolitionists including Senator Charles Sumner of Massachusetts and Representative Thaddeus Stevens of Pennsylvania. The Radicals believed that the federal government had a responsibility to protect the rights of the freedpeople. They argued that Reconstruction must involve broad social and political changes in the South, in order to ensure that the former slaves remained truly free from their former masters. "There is one, and only one, sure and safe policy for the immediate future," argued the Radical newspaper the *Independent*. "The North must remain the absolute Dictator of the Republic until the spirit of the North shall become the spirit of the whole country."

Thaddeus Stevens was a gifted speech maker and a passionate defender of African Americans' rights. When he died in 1868, ten thousand freedmen attended his funeral.

In July 1864 Congress passed a Radical alternative to President Lincoln's Reconstruction plan, known as the Wade-Davis Bill. The bill required at least 50 percent of a state's voters to pledge their loyalty to the Union before the state could reestablish its government. The new Southern governments had to not only abolish slavery but also guarantee African Americans equality under the law. In addition, the Wade-Davis Bill included strict penalties for former Confederates. Southerners would not be allowed to vote or hold office until they took an oath that

"WHAT THE BLACK MAN WANTS"

One of the leading spokespersons for African-American rights during the Reconstruction era was Frederick Douglass. Born a slave in 1818, Douglass had escaped to freedom as a young man. He joined the abolitionist movement and became a famous writer, speaker, and newspaper publisher. A few days before the end of

Freedmen line up to cast their ballots in Richmond, Virginia, in 1871.

the Civil War, Douglass gave a speech called "What the Black Man Wants," in which he explained the importance of enfranchisement (voting rights) to the freedpeople.

> I am for the "immediate, unconditional, and universal" enfranchisement of the black man, in every State in the Union. Without this, his liberty is a mockery; without this, you might as well almost retain the old name of slavery for his condition; for in fact, if he is not the slave of the individual master, he is the slave of society, and holds his liberty as a privilege, not as a right. He is at the mercy of the mob, and has no means of protecting himself.
>
> We want [the vote] because it is our right, first of all. No class of men can, without insulting their own nature, be content with any deprivation of their rights. . . . I want the elective franchise, for one, as a colored man, because ours is a peculiar government, based upon a peculiar idea, and that idea is universal suffrage. . . . [H]ere where universal suffrage is the rule, where that is the fundamental idea of the Government, to rule us out is to make us an exception, to brand us with the stigma [mark] of inferiority, and to invite to our heads the missiles of those about us.

they had never supported the Confederacy in any way. Any person who continued to support the Confederacy after the bill became law would be "declared not to be a citizen of the United States."

Lincoln considered the Wade-Davis Bill harsh and impractical. He used a pocket veto—"pocketing" the unsigned bill until Congress adjourned—to make certain that it would not become law. Radical leaders were furious. Over the following months, the president and Congress would continue to wrestle for control over the course of Reconstruction.

THE PRESIDENT TESTS HIS PLAN

While the cannons roared, President Lincoln had an advantage over his opponents in Congress. As commander in chief of Union forces in the South, he could appoint military governors to the occupied Confederate states. He could use those officials to put some of his ideas for Reconstruction into action.

In 1864 Lincoln chose the Union-occupied Confederate state of Louisiana as the testing ground for his Ten Percent Plan. He had appointed General Nathaniel Banks as military commander of Louisiana. Banks administered the oath of loyalty to 12,000 of the state's voters, and the president granted them a presidential pardon. Then Lincoln ordered the general to hold elections, so that the citizens could choose delegates to a constitutional convention. At the convention the delegates drafted a new constitution abolishing slavery. The constitution also gave the Louisiana state legislature the power to grant limited voting rights to blacks.

Lincoln was encouraged by these developments. However,

Union general Nathaniel P. Banks reorganized the Louisiana state government under President Lincoln's moderate Reconstruction plan.

his experiment in political Reconstruction was soon in jeopardy. Louisiana's newly elected legislature refused to grant African Americans their voting rights. In turn, Congress refused to recognize the reconstructed state. The president urged congressional leaders to reconsider, arguing that black men would gain the vote more quickly "by saving the already advanced steps toward it, than by running backward over them. . . . The new government of Louisiana is only to what it should be as the egg is to the fowl; we shall sooner have the fowl by hatching the egg than by smashing it."

Despite the president's pleas, the experiment in reorganizing Louisiana's government ended in disappointment. Congress stuck to its decision. Making matters even worse, supporters of slavery soon gained control of the state's new government. The failure of Lincoln's generous Ten Percent Plan convinced many Northerners that more radical forms of Reconstruction would be needed.

THE SEA ISLAND EXPERIMENT

While the Louisiana experiment concentrated on politics, there was far more to Reconstruction than simply reestablishing Southern state governments. Other wartime rehearsals for Reconstruction tackled the deeper problems of reshaping an entire society based on slave labor. The most ambitious of these experiments took place on the Sea Islands off the coast of South Carolina.

When Union forces occupied the Sea Islands in November 1861, most of the white residents fled, leaving behind about ten thousand slaves. Northern abolitionists and military officers seized this opportunity to create a new society that would become a showcase for freedom. Teachers and missionaries opened schools to educate the former slaves. Federal officials and private investors hired the newly freed laborers to work on the abandoned plantations for wages. The government also set aside 16,000 acres of land, which was divided into small lots and offered to black residents for $1.25 an acre.

The Sea Island experiment was a mixture of successes and failures. The freedmen's schools gave thousands of black men, women, and children their first chance at an education. African Americans also tasted the freedom of earning wages, controlling their personal lives, and raising their families without interference from white masters. A few former slaves even realized their dreams of owning their own farms. However, most of the islands' black residents could not afford even the low prices charged for the government-owned lots. Some poor farmers settled on abandoned plantations, where they raised crops in the hopes of earning enough money to buy the land. Eventually, these "squatters" were driven off by the government, which sold their farms to wealthy white investors. The majority of black laborers ended up working for white landowners, under conditions not much different from their lives under slavery.

In 1864 a group of nineteen Sea Island laborers wrote to President Lincoln. The freedmen and women worked for Edward Philbrick, a Boston abolitionist who had moved to the islands and bought several abandoned plantations. Philbrick hoped to prove that African Americans could be more productive as free wage earners than as slave laborers. He paid his workers low wages and maintained strict discipline in order to achieve his goal. "Wee hav work'd for Mr Philbrick the whole year faithfully," the laborers told the president, "and hav

A manager weighs cotton picked by black laborers on a Reconstruction-era plantation.

received nothing comparatively, not enough to sustaine life if wee depended entirely uppon our wages." In addition, some of Philbrick's managers used harsh punishments. One young girl was "turned . . . over a Barrel, & whip'd . . . with a Leathern Strap." While such brutalities had been common under slavery, the freedpeople were dismayed to find them continuing after emancipation. Their first experiences of "free labor," they wrote, had left them "discouraged, all most heart broken."

FINAL DAYS

Even as President Lincoln and congressional leaders argued over Reconstruction policies, they managed to work together on several key measures protecting African-American rights. One of the most important of these measures was the Thirteenth Amendment to the Constitution.

The Emancipation Proclamation had left many African Americans in slavery in the loyal border states (slaveholding states on the border between North and South that had remained loyal to the Union). The Thirteenth Amendment went further, calling for the abolition of slavery throughout the nation. Lincoln worked with Radical Republicans to push the controversial amendment through Congress in January 1865. Then he incorporated it into his Reconstruction plan. The new Southern state governments formed under the Ten Percent Plan would have to approve the Thirteenth Amendment before rejoining the Union.

Another important wartime measure authorized the creation of a federal agency to help former slaves make the transition from slavery to freedom. The Bureau of Refugees, Freedmen, and Abandoned Lands, commonly known as the Freedmen's Bureau, would be the first federal agency ever created to aid and protect individual Americans. Congress passed the bill establishing the Freedmen's Bureau on March 3, 1865. Within a few hours, the president had signed it into law.

On April 9 the Confederate army surrendered, ending the Civil War. Addressing the joyous crowd that gathered outside the White House, the president discussed some of the complex issues of Reconstruction. In his speech he endorsed the idea of voting rights for black Americans. Lincoln's proposal limited suffrage to "the very intelligent, and . . . those who serve our cause as soldiers." Nevertheless, it was the first time any American president had ever called for granting African Americans the vote.

Lincoln's statements outraged at least one member of his audience. John Wilkes Booth, an actor and a fanatical Confederate sympathizer, vowed, "That is the last speech he will make." On April 14 Booth carried out his threat, shooting and fatally wounding Abraham Lincoln. With the assassination of the president, the many challenges and opportunities of Reconstruction passed into other hands.

Andrew Johnson takes the oath of office as America's seventeenth president following the assassination of Abraham Lincoln.

Chapter 2

A New and Stubborn War

WITHIN HOURS OF ABRAHAM LINCOLN'S DEATH ON April 15, 1865, Vice President Andrew Johnson was sworn in as president. Johnson was a proud man with a humble background. He had grown up in poverty in North Carolina, where he had been a tailor's apprentice. Moving to Tennessee, he had worked his way up to become a successful farmer and the owner of five slaves. A spectacular career in politics had taken him all the way from the Tennessee state legislature to the governor's office to the U.S. Senate. During the Civil War, Johnson was the only senator from a Confederate state who remained in Congress. Although he was a Democrat, his loyalty to the Union had earned him the Republican nomination as President Lincoln's running mate in the election of 1864.

Radical Republicans who had opposed Lincoln's generous Reconstruction policies were pleased with his replacement.

Johnson had made it clear that he despised the high and mighty class of Southern plantation owners. He had denounced former Confederate leaders as "traitors" who should be "tried, convicted, and hanged." Senator Benjamin Wade, the Radical coauthor of the Wade-Davis Bill, expressed confidence that Johnson would "deal with these damned rebels . . . according to their deserts."

African Americans, however, were uncertain what to expect from the new president. Speaking to an audience of freedmen in early 1864, the former slaveholder had vowed, "I will indeed be your Moses, and lead you through the Red Sea of war and bondage to a fairer future of liberty and peace." On the other hand, it sometimes seemed that Johnson had turned against slavery mainly because he believed that it was bad for poor whites. In supporting abolition in his home state, he had explained that he favored emancipation "for two reasons: first, because it is right in itself; and second, because in the emanci-

Andrew Johnson's tailor shop in Greeneville, Tennessee. Johnson's humble beginnings left him bitter and resentful toward wealthy plantation owners.

pation of the slaves, we break down an odious and dangerous aristocracy; I think that we are freeing more whites than blacks in Tennessee."

PRESIDENTIAL RECONSTRUCTION

President Johnson wasted no time outlining his plans for restoring the union. Six weeks after becoming president, while Congress was in recess, he issued two proclamations. These pronouncements marked the beginning of a period known as Presidential Reconstruction, which would last from 1865 to 1867. The first proclamation offered an amnesty to former Confederates who took an oath pledging their loyalty to the Union and their support of emancipation. All property except slaves would be restored to those who were pardoned. The amnesty excluded high-ranking Confederate political and military leaders as well as wealthy Southerners who owned property worth more than $20,000. Those men would have to apply personally to the president for a special pardon.

The second proclamation provided for the political reorganization of the former Confederate states. The president would appoint provisional (temporary) governors, who would oversee the election of delegates to constitutional conventions. After the states drafted their new constitutions, elections would be held for government offices. The newly organized governments would have to renounce secession and ratify the Thirteenth Amendment, abolishing slavery. Except for those requirements, they would be largely free to manage their own affairs, including any measures taken to protect the newly freed slaves.

White Southerners were delighted with the easy terms of President Johnson's Reconstruction plan. Thousands of

President Johnson pardons former Confederates at the White House. Johnson would eventually grant more than 13,500 special presidential pardons.

wealthy plantation owners flocked to the White House, seeking the special presidential pardon. Observers reported that Johnson relished the sight of rich and powerful planters begging for his forgiveness. After all his talk of harsh punishments, it seemed that the former tailor was mainly concerned with humiliating the proud aristocrats who had once looked down on him.

Catherine Ann Devereux Edmondston, the wife of a wealthy North Carolina planter, described the Confederates' view of President Johnson's policies. Several members of Edmondston's family had "asked & received pardon at the hand of his high mightiness Andy Johnson for the crime of being worth more than $20,000." Despite their embarrassment, Edmondston wrote, the pardoned Southerners would have the last laugh. "Not one person whom I have heard speak of [the loyalty oath] but laughs at and repudiates [rejects] every obligation it imposes."

RETURN OF THE REBELS

During the summer and fall of 1865, white Southerners reorganized their governments under President Johnson's Reconstruction plan. African Americans played no role in the process. Under Southern laws they were not allowed to vote. Only white males took part in the constitutional conventions, and only white males were elected to office. Dozens of former Confederate leaders returned to power in local and state offices and the U.S. Congress.

One of the first tasks of the newly elected state legislatures was to pass laws defining the rights and responsibilities of the emancipated slaves. Some of this legislation was reasonable. New laws gave the freedpeople the right to sign contracts, get married, and sue in the courts. However, a large body of laws severely restricted African Americans' political, social, and economic rights. These laws came to be known as the Black Codes.

The Black Codes varied from state to state, but most contained the same kinds of restrictions. The majority of the laws concerned labor. Some labor laws dictated the relations between black workers and white planters. These codes were designed to ensure that African Americans continued to work under the strict control of their former masters or other white employers. Vagrancy laws made it a crime for able-bodied black adults to be unemployed. Men and women who were declared vagrants could be arrested and sentenced to a period of hard labor. Apprenticing laws gave the courts broad powers to hire out black children to white employers, often their former owners. Other labor laws barred African Americans from all but the most menial occupations. In Mississippi and South Carolina, for example, former slaves were only allowed to work as field hands or servants, unless they paid a steep fee and obtained a special license.

The Black Codes also imposed racial segregation and other forms of discrimination. African Americans were forbidden to vote, sit on juries, testify against whites, own weapons, or serve in state militias. They could be punished more severely than whites for the same crimes. In Louisiana local laws made it almost impossible for blacks to live in large towns or cities without permission from white employers. In Florida a "person of color" who entered "any railroad-car or other vehicle set apart for the accommodation of white persons" could be "whipped with thirty-nine lashes on the bare back." In addition, most states passed laws forbidding interracial marriages. An African American who married a white person in Alabama could be sentenced to seven years in prison. In Mississippi the penalty was life imprisonment.

COMBATING THE CODES

Many white Northerners were prejudiced against blacks, and many Northern states had laws allowing segregation and other forms of discrimination. Nevertheless, the people of the North loudly condemned the Black Codes. The Southern laws were clearly meant to overturn one of the main results of the Civil War, the ending of slavery. To Northerners, that was an insult to the hundreds of thousands of soldiers who had fought and died for Union victory. Northerners were also horrified that former Confederate leaders were returning to office instead of facing prosecution as traitors to the Union. Northern Republican leaders had another reason for opposing the Black Codes. They knew that African-American men who were granted the

BLACK CODES OF MISSISSIPPI

Mississippi passed some of the first and harshest Black Codes. Here are excerpts from laws passed by the Mississippi state legislature in November 1865.

White Americans unite to deny blacks their rights and freedoms, in this political cartoon by Thomas Nast.

[It] shall not be lawful for any freedman, free negro or mulatto [a person of mixed white and black ancestry] to intermarry with any white person; . . . and any person who shall so intermarry shall be deemed guilty of felony, and on conviction thereof shall be confined in the State penitentiary for life.

Every civil officer shall, and every person may, arrest and carry back to his or her legal employer any freedman, free negro, or mulatto who shall have quit the service of his or her employer before the expiration of his or her term of service without good cause.

It shall be the duty of all sheriffs, justices of the peace, and other civil officers of the several counties in this State, to report . . . all freedmen, free negroes, and mulattoes, under the age of eighteen, . . . who are orphans, or whose parent or parents have not the means or who refuse to provide for and support said minors; and thereupon it shall be the duty of [the court] to apprentice said minors to some competent and suitable person. In the management and control of said apprentices, said master or mistress shall have the power to inflict such moderate corporeal chastisement [physical punishment] as a father or guardian is allowed to inflict on his or her child.

All freedmen, free negroes and mulattoes in this State, over the age of eighteen years, found . . . with no lawful employment or business, or found unlawfully assembling themselves together, either in the day or night time, . . . shall be deemed vagrants, and on conviction thereof shall be fined . . . and imprisoned.

A family of cotton pickers in Georgia. For many former slaves, working conditions during Reconstruction were not much better than they had been under slavery.

vote would overwhelmingly choose the party of Abraham Lincoln and emancipation over the Democratic Party of their former masters. That would ensure that the Republicans remained in control of Congress.

While white Northerners denounced the return of the slaveholding powers, African Americans watched their dreams of true freedom fade away. "Freedom wasn't no difference I knows of," recalled one former slave. "I works for Marse John just the same." James Green, a field hand in Texas, saw "no big change" on the ranch where he lived and worked in constant dread of his cruel master. The freedpeople lived in "de same houses and some got whipped," he said, although "nobody got nailed to a tree by de ears, like dey used to."

Former slaves throughout the South sent petitions to their state governments and Congress, protesting the Black Codes. One petition from African Americans in Norfolk, Virginia, asserted that the old arguments in support of slavery "have by no means faded from the minds of the people of the South; they cling to these delusions still, and only hug them closer for their recent defeat. Worse than all, they have returned to their homes, with all their old pride and contempt for the Negro transformed into bitter hate for the new-made freeman."

In some Southern states, African Americans organized

THE RECONSTRUCTION ERA

political conventions to discuss ways to combat the unjust laws. The Colored People's Convention of South Carolina issued this appeal to the state's white citizens:

> We ask for no special privileges or peculiar favors. We ask only for *even-handed Justice,* or for the removal of such positive obstructions and disabilities as past, and the recent Legislators have seen fit to throw in our way, and heap upon us. . . .
>
> We simply desire that we shall be recognized as men; that we have no obstructions placed in our way; that the same laws which govern white men shall direct colored men; that we have the right of trial by a jury of our peers, that schools be opened or established for our children; that we be permitted to acquire homesteads for ourselves and children; that we be dealt with as others, in equity and justice.

Despite such appeals, the hard-won freedoms of the former slaves would continue to erode. For many Southern blacks, life in the Reconstruction era would become a constant struggle against poverty and injustice. The end of the Civil War, proclaimed the black abolitionist leader Henry H. Garnet, had plunged African Americans into another "stubborn war with unrelenting foes, which we mean to fight to the end on our native soil, aiming to complete the establishment of our rights and liberties."

Millions of former
slaves like this Georgia
couple struggled against
poverty and oppression
in Reconstruction times.

Chapter 3

From Slavery to Free Labor

"SOMETIMES I GITS ALONG TOLERABLE; SOMETIMES right slim," said a freedwoman in Atlanta in 1865. "[B]ut dat's de way wid everybody—times is powerful hard right now."

In the weeks and months following the end of the Civil War, former slaves asserted their newfound freedom. For the first time in their lives, they could come and go as they pleased. Vast numbers of freedpeople walked off the plantations with little more than a bundle of belongings slung across their backs. Some headed to towns and cities, where they hoped to find good jobs and better lives for themselves and their children. Most stayed in the more familiar countryside, often within a few miles of their old homes. Wherever they traveled, remembered former slave Felix Haywood, the freedpeople "seemed to want to get closer to freedom, so they'd know what it was—like it was a place."

General Oliver Otis Howard became commissioner of the Freedmen's Bureau in 1865. This photo was taken a few years earlier by the famous American photographer Mathew Brady.

Times were hard for nearly everyone in the war-ravaged South, but former slaves bore an added burden. Wherever they turned, they ran into opposition from their former masters. Defeated but defiant, whites were determined to use every means possible to regain control of the South's black population.

In these perilous times, African Americans had at least one ally: the Freedmen's Bureau. Shortly before his death, President Lincoln had chosen General Oliver Otis Howard to head the new agency. Howard assigned assistant commissioners to oversee specific regions of the South and local agents to supervise districts within those regions. The agents would be responsible for aiding and protecting the freedpeople during their journey from slavery to citizenship.

FORTY ACRES AND A MULE

For many former slaves, true freedom meant owning a piece of land, where they could grow their own crops, build their own homes, and escape from a lifetime of control by white masters. "Gib us our own land and we take care [of] ourselves," explained a South Carolina freedman, "but widout land, de ole masses [masters] can hire us or starve us, as dey please." A black army veteran agreed. "Every colored man will be a slave & feel himself a slave," he said, "until he can raise him own bale of cotton & put him own mark upon it & say dis is mine!"

At first, it seemed that those dreams of land ownership

might come true. A few months before the war's end, Union general William T. Sherman had issued an order setting aside a strip of land stretching from Charleston, South Carolina, to Jacksonville, Florida, for black settlement. Each family would receive forty acres of farmland carved from abandoned Confederate plantations. The army would even lend black farmers mules to work their fields. By June 1865, about 40,000 former slaves had settled on the confiscated lands. Hopes soared as rumors swept the South: the government planned to give every former slave "forty acres and a mule"!

President Johnson's proclamation of amnesty shattered those hopes. During the summer and fall of 1865, former Confederates who had received presidential pardons returned to reclaim their prewar property. African Americans had been settling on abandoned lands all across the South, and many refused to leave their farms. "We has a right to the land where we are located," argued Bayley Wyat, a freedman living on a farm near Yorktown, Virginia. "For why? I tell you. Our wives, our children, our husbands, has been sold over and over again to purchase the lands we now locates upon."

At first, the Freedmen's Bureau sided with black farmers. The president soon put an end to the resistance, however, ordering the bureau to return all confiscated lands to the former owners. Federal troops eventually evicted the remaining freedpeople from their farms. While a few former slaves managed to buy their own land, the vast majority found it impossible. Most were desperately poor. Even those who had money could rarely find a white landowner who was willing to sell to them. In the face of all these obstacles, most former slaves had no choice: they had to return to work for their former masters.

PICKLED HORSE AND CRACKERS

Members of a poor country family pose outside their cabin in Kentucky around 1870.

A few former slaves defied the odds and realized their dreams of land ownership. One of these determined individuals was Mattie Curtis. Mattie had spent the Civil War years in North Carolina, where she was enslaved by a foul-tempered mistress who sometimes whipped her until her back ran with blood. Shortly before the war's end, a Union soldier brought a ray of hope. The man rode up to the plantation, Mattie remembered, and "he tels us dat de lan' wus goin' ter be cut up an' divided among de slaves, dey would also have a mule an' a house apiece." When freedom came at last, however, the promise of land proved false. "I always had craved a home an' a plenty to eat," said Mattie, "but freedom ain't gib us notin' but pickled hoss meat an' dirty crackers, an' not half enough of dat."

Discouraged but not beaten, Mattie bought fifteen acres of land "on time," agreeing to pay for it with the money she made from crops. Almost single-handedly she cleared her property of trees and brush, plowed the fields, and planted cotton. She "done a heap of work at night too," caring for her home and raising nineteen children. At last, Mattie managed to pay for the land. The proud woman continued to work on her farm for many years. When she reached her eighties, she finally decided to hire a strong young laborer to help in the fields. Mattie soon concluded that the "young generation ain't worth shucks. . . . [Be]fore leben o'clock he passed out on me."

A New Labor System

The costs of war and the collapse of the slave-based labor system had left the Southern economy in ruins. In order for the region to recover, it was essential for plantations to become productive again. The plantation owners needed laborers. The freedpeople needed jobs. However, Southern whites were determined to regain complete control over their workers, while African Americans were equally resolved to defend their freedom and independence. The challenging job of resolving those conflicts fell to the Freedmen's Bureau.

The bureau met the challenge by requiring or encouraging workers and employers to sign labor contracts. Labor contracts had been introduced by Union commanders during the Civil War. Under this system former slaves signed contracts in which they agreed to work for a planter or other white employer for one year. The contracts specified the terms of employment, including the workers' duties, hours, and pay. Payment might be in the form of wages or a share of the harvest, and it often included food, lodging, and sometimes clothing and medical care.

While labor contracts were intended to restore production and protect black laborers, white planters soon found ways to use the system to their advantage. Under the Black Codes, labor contracts returned the freedpeople to a state close to slavery. Laborers were often forbidden to leave the plantations or receive visitors without their employers' permission. Planters could impose fines or physical punishments for employees who were "disrespectful" or "disobedient." Blacks who left their employers before their contracts expired could be whipped, placed in the stocks (a wooden plank with holes for the ankles or wrists), or sold at auction for up to a year of hard labor. Many

A white Southerner prepares to whip a shirtless black man. The platform above the whipping post holds the stocks.

employers added their own touches to these legal provisions. One planter inserted a line in his labor contracts requiring black workers to address him as "master." Another insisted that his employees obey his orders "strictly as my slaves." Planters also used complicated language to take advantage of the former slaves' inexperience with free labor. On one plantation field hands contracted to work for a year in exchange for "one third of seven twelfths of the crop."

Freedmen's Bureau agents helped workers negotiate better contracts, with more reasonable wages and fewer restrictions. They also settled disputes between black workers and their employers. George A. Harmount, an assistant superintendent in Alabama, saw cases every day "of persons refusing to pay Negroes the wages agreed upon—and yet these contracts have been made in my office. The people here feel indignant that they are obliged to hire the Negroes they used to own, and will by every possible means endeavor to evade the payment of wages due them."

Despite the efforts of the Freedmen's Bureau, conflicts and abuses continued. The overworked agents could not possibly ensure that all labor contracts were fair. In addition, in trying to satisfy both white planters and black workers, many Northern white agents were influenced by their own racial prejudices. Well-meaning agents often urged former slaves to prove themselves "worthy" of freedom by working hard and faithfully for their former masters. A Northern reporter who stud-

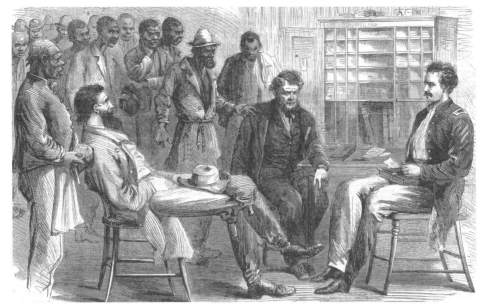

White employers and black employees negotiated labor contracts at Freedmen's Bureau offices. This illustration makes it clear which group typically had the upper hand.

ied Southern labor relations observed that the bureau was supposed to be "the next friend of the blacks [but] it appears to stand too often as their next enemy." After watching one agent at work in South Carolina, the reporter wrote, "He doesn't really intend to outrage the rights of the negroes, but he has very little idea that they have any rights except such as the planters choose to give them."

WORKING FOR SHARES

For most black agricultural workers, the wage labor system proved to be too much like slavery. They lived in the same run-down "slave cabins." They did the same work, under basically the same conditions. Often that meant working in chain gangs, under the watchful eyes of white planters and overseers. Longing to escape white domination but unable to buy their own land, many former slaves turned to sharecropping.

Under a typical sharecropping arrangement, a black worker signed a contract that gave his family responsibility for a small

A sharecropper collects his meager earnings for a delivery of cotton.

plot of land owned by a white planter. The planter supplied seed, livestock, tools, and other farm supplies. The sharecropper planted and raised cotton, tobacco, or other crops. The crops were turned over to the landowner, who sold them and gave the cropper a share of the profits, after deducting the cost of the supplies and various other expenses.

The sharecropping system worked well for plantation owners. Money for wages was scarce in the postwar South, and the system ensured landowners a cheap and reliable labor force. For black farmers, however, sharecropping was a tragic failure. During the planting season, sharecroppers had to buy their food, clothing, fuel, and other supplies on credit from the plantation store or local white merchants. Bad weather could mean a poor harvest, leaving farmers with nothing to pay their debts.

In addition, planters found many ways to cheat croppers out of their shares. They inflated the prices of the goods they sold, and they deducted so much for expenses that there were no profits left to divide after the crops went to market. Many sharecroppers fell so deeply in debt that they were practically re-enslaved.

"We made crops on share for three years after freedom," recalled Richard Crump of Mississippi. "They didn't pay everything they promised. They taken a lot of it away from us. They said figures didn't lie." Former slave Henry Blake described a similar experience. After emancipation Henry and his parents worked as sharecroppers for white planters in Arkansas.

> We couldn't make nothing—just overalls and something to eat. A man that didn't know how to count would always lose. He might lose anyhow. They didn't give no itemized statement [bill]. No, you just had to take their word. They never give you no details. They just say you owe so much. No matter how good account you kept, you had to go by their account and now, Brother, I'm tellin' you the truth about this. . . . He was always right and you was always wrong.

Chapter 4

HOPES, HEARTBREAK, AND OUTRAGES

IN AUGUST 1865 AN AFRICAN-AMERICAN SOLDIER reported that the freedpeople in Kansas and Missouri were "all most Thread less & shoeless without food & no home. . . . [Several] of there Masters Run them off & as fur as I can see the hole Race will fall back if the U.S. Goverment dont pervid [provide] for them Some way or ruther."

The government did provide. That summer the Freedmen's Bureau distributed about 150,000 daily rations of food to Southern refugees, with about one-third going to poor whites and two-thirds to African Americans. By 1870, the number of rations issued would climb to nearly 22 million. In addition, the bureau distributed clothing and operated refugee camps for homeless Southerners, white and black.

Other social services were designed to help the former slaves adjust to their new lives. Freedmen's Bureau agents

Opposite: Southern whites burn a freedmen's school in Memphis, Tennessee.

helped black communities found schools and churches. They provided assistance to freedpeople who were struggling to restore their families. The bureau also tried to protect Southern blacks from intimidation and violence.

A Hunger for Education

Before the war every Southern state except Tennessee had laws against teaching slaves to read and write. As a result, the vast majority of former slaves were illiterate. The freedpeople knew that education was one of their most important tools for raising themselves out of poverty and dependence. "If I nebber does do nothing more while I live," said one Mississippi freedman, "I shall give my children a chance to go to school, for I considers education next best ting to liberty." A former slave in Louisiana observed that even after emancipation, whites continued to use their "book-larning" to take advantage of blacks. It was more important to give children an education than a fortune, he asserted, "because if you left them even five hundred dollars, some man having more education than they had would come along and cheat them out of it."

To satisfy this hunger for education, the Freedmen's Bureau worked with Northern aid societies to build, furnish, and oversee hundreds of freedmen's schools. The agency also provided transportation for the thousands of teachers, white and black, who came south to work with the freedpeople.

One of the main forces behind the growth of the freedmen's schools, however, was the freedpeople themselves. In many parts of the South, black communities pooled their resources to build schoolhouses and hire teachers. Where money was scarce, families might pay a teacher's salary with eggs, vegeta-

Student teachers practice working with young children at Fisk University in Nashville, Tennessee.

bles, and other farm produce. One black teacher in Virginia reported that she had received "5 eggs and a chicken" as tuition. The freedpeople also joined forces to protect their teachers and schools from attacks by white neighbors who opposed black education. In some areas freedmen stood guard in shifts, day and night, outside their schoolhouses.

Hundreds of thousands of African Americans, adults and children alike, attended the freedmen's schools. Many students came in the evening, after a long day of labor. "The children . . . hurry to school as soon as their work is over," wrote a teacher in Norfolk, Virginia. "The plowmen hurry from the field at night to get their hour of study. Old men and women strain their dim sight . . . to catch the shape of the letter."

In addition to the freedmen's schools, the Reconstruction era saw the opening of the nation's first black colleges. These schools of higher learning included Fisk University in Tennessee, Hampton Normal and Agricultural Institute in Virginia, and Howard University in Washington, DC. While black colleges offered a variety of courses, many students trained to become teachers. By 1870, about half of the nine thousand teachers in freedmen's schools were African Americans.

THE FREEDOM TO WORSHIP

Black communities often built churches alongside their new schools, or they built churches that doubled as houses of worship and freedmen's schools. A number of churches were established with the help of the Freedmen's Bureau and Northern missionary societies. Others were built with funds raised by the freedpeople themselves.

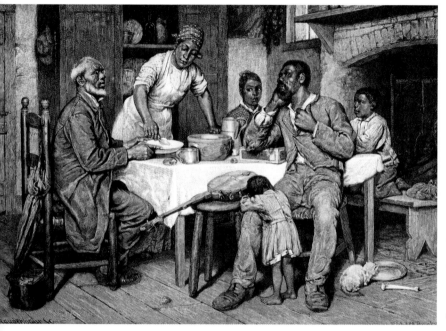

A black preacher visits church members. Emancipation gave Southern blacks their first chance to found their own churches and choose their own preachers.

Under slavery, black worshippers had been second-class members of white churches. Seated in the back pews or the gallery overlooking white worshippers, they listened as white ministers preached the virtues of service and obedience to the slave masters. "When the white preacher come," recalled one freedman, "he preach and pick up his Bible and claim he gittin the text right out from the good Book and he preach: 'The Lord say, don't you [blacks] steal chickens from your missus. Don't you steal your marster's hawgs.' That wuld be all he preach." Former slave Susan Boggs was also skeptical of white preachers, many of whom were slaveholders themselves. "The man that baptized me," she said, "had a colored woman tied up in his yard to whip when he got home, that very Sunday."

During Reconstruction, African Americans were free to hire their own preachers and worship without white interference. Their new churches served not only as houses of worship but also as the headquarters for black social groups, aid societies, and political organizations. In time the independent black church would become the vibrant center of the social, political, and economic life of the African-American community.

FAMILY TIES

Before the Civil War, Southern laws had not recognized marriages between slaves. After emancipation many black couples were eager to legalize their "slave marriages." Mass wedding ceremonies involving as many as seventy couples at a time took place at Freedmen's Bureau offices.

African-American couples were denied legal marriages under slavery. These newly freed slaves are taking part in a mass wedding ceremony.

Slavery had also torn apart families, as slaveholders sold husbands away from wives, children away from parents. In the months following the war, thousands of freedpeople set out to find their lost relatives. The searchers traveled to the places where a wife or child had last been seen. They followed rumors and inquired at black schools and churches. One Northern journalist met a former slave who had walked more than six hundred miles from Georgia to North Carolina. "Plodding along, staff in hand, and apparently very footsore and tired," the man was seeking the wife and children he had been sold away from four years earlier.

Former slaves who could not travel placed ads in black newspapers, describing a loved one and asking for information on the missing person's whereabouts. Many freedpeople also turned to the Freedmen's Bureau. The bureau served as a clearinghouse of information about missing persons. In addition, local agents tracked down slave traders, searched sales records, and wrote thousands of letters to help searchers follow their leads. In some cases the agency provided transportation to reunite separated families.

Sadly, most searches for lost relatives ended in heartbreak. A woman might learn that her missing parents had died. A man might track down his wife only to find that she had remarried.

The main office of the Virginia Freedmen's Bureau was located in Richmond, former capital of the Confederacy.

THE CASE OF ALICE MOORE

Many Freedmen's Bureau agents did their best to help freedmen and women reunite their families. Despite their efforts and the determination of African Americans to find missing loved ones, most searches were unsuccessful. The case of Alice Moore is typical of the many sad stories found in bureau records.

Alice was fifteen years old when she was sold away from her family in North Carolina to a new master in Virginia. The following year, the war ended, and she began a long search for her missing parents. In May 1865 Alice went to the Freedmen's Bureau office in Staunton, Virginia. She

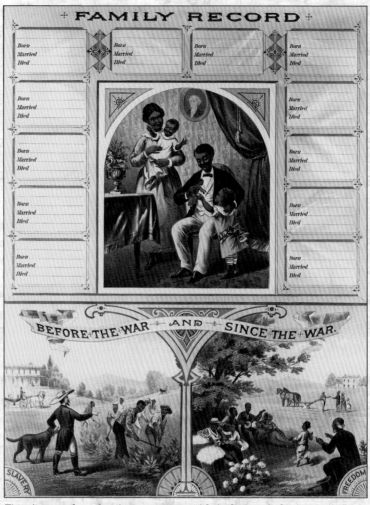

This diagram for a family tree contrasts life before and after emancipation.

gave the agents descriptions of her mother and father and the addresses of the plantations where they had lived. Alice's case was passed along to the Virginia state headquarters, to the national office in Washington, DC, and then to several North Carolina agencies. Her parents were traced as far as New Berne, North Carolina. There the trail went cold. In July 1867 the New Berne agency reported that, "although diligent Search and inquiry [had] been made," no trace of the missing couple could be found. As far as we know, Alice Moore was never reunited with her parents.

Children who had been separated from their families at a young age might feel confused and frightened when a strange man or woman appeared, claiming to be their father or mother. Most often, freedmen and women were forced to give up their quests after months of fruitless searching. The records of slave sales were incomplete, and searchers often had little more to guide them than a name and physical description, which was likely to be outdated and inaccurate after a long separation. Twenty years after the war's end, black newspapers were still filled with ads from former slaves seeking long-lost loved ones.

Along with all these disappointments came the occasional happy ending. Against all odds, families that had been torn apart by slavery were sometimes joyfully reunited. One mother visiting a refugee camp in Virginia found her eighteen-year-old daughter, who had been sold away from her in infancy. A young woman from Mississippi took her three children on a long journey to Virginia, where she found her missing father. An elderly couple named Ben and Betsy Dodson were reunited at a refugee camp twenty years after their master sold them apart. "Glory! glory! hallelujah," the jubilant husband shouted as he embraced his wife. "Dis is my Betty, shuah. I foun' you at las'."

VIOLENCE AND INJUSTICE

After the Civil War, violence continued to plague the South. White Southerners resented the loss of their slaves, and many took out their anger in vicious attacks on the freedpeople. Often these assaults had an underlying purpose: to punish former slaves who violated traditional Southern customs of white supremacy and black submission.

White Southerners whip a black girl in 1867. Over time violent attacks on the freedpeople would become increasingly widespread and brutal.

Freedpeople were whipped or beaten for speaking "disre-spectfully" to whites, refusing to step aside on city sidewalks, or arguing with their employers over wages or working conditions. They were murdered for sending their children to school or trying to buy their own farms. An elderly black man in Tennessee "got his head split open with an axe" after he "sassed" a white man. In Louisiana a freedman was shot for refusing to take off his hat in the presence of his former master. In South Carolina a white planter sent armed gunmen after a husband and wife who had refused to sign a lifetime labor contract. The freedman was shot and killed. The woman received "fifty lashes upon the bare back," after which she was tormented for a week, forced to plow by day and locked in a dark cell at night, with nothing to eat. She was finally rescued by an officer of the Freedmen's Bureau.

Charles Watkins, an African-American veteran, wrote to Freedmen's Bureau commissioner Oliver Otis Howard about assaults on the freedpeople of Queen Anne's County, Maryland.

> [The] returned colard Solgers are in Many cases beten, and their guns taken from them, we darcent [don't dare] walk out of an evening if we do, and we are Met by Some of these roudies that were in the rebbel army they beat us badly and Sumtime Shoot us. . . . our collard School teacher was . . . beaten, he got loos and ran and was Shot at. . . . on Sunday evening the 11th Sum persons . . . cam on horse back [and] Set fier to the chirch that we keep School in and burnt it to the ground. Now—Sir— this is the way we get our freedom can you do any thing for us. for gods Sake do it

Each month local Freedmen's Bureau offices sent reports of similar incidents to agency headquarters in Washington, DC. There was little the bureau could do, however, to help the victims of racial violence. Overworked local agents were stretched too thin to address the widespread problem. Some were more worried about offending white Southern authorities than protecting defenseless black people.

Agents who did try to help usually ran into powerful opposition from local courts and law officers. While African Americans were arrested for the most trivial offenses, whites who committed crimes against blacks were almost never punished. The Black Codes barred African Americans from juries, and white juries and judges nearly always ignored testimony from black witnesses. A federal official in Georgia observed that "no jury would convict a white man for killing a freedman, or fail to hang a negro who had killed a white man in self-defense." A Georgia freedman agreed. "Should anyone think that with the freedom of the black man has come equal justice," he wrote, "let him come to Macon and visit the Mayor's court and he will see his mistake. A white may assault a colored gentleman at high noon, pelt him with stones or maul him with a club and the colored man is fined or imprisoned."

Chapter 5

THE RECONSTRUCTION GOVERNMENTS

BY THE END OF 1865, ALL OF THE FORMER CONFEDERATE states had reorganized under President Johnson's Reconstruction plan. While the new state governments had reluctantly recognized emancipation, they refused to protect the rights of the freedpeople. Former Confederate leaders were back in power. Emboldened by the president's hands-off policies, they had resumed their defiance of Northern "interference" in Southern affairs. Intimidation, violence, and the discriminatory Black Codes had returned the freedpeople to a status close to slavery.

On December 4 President Johnson announced that loyal governments were functioning throughout the South and Reconstruction was complete. Republican lawmakers were quick to disagree. The stage was set for a heated battle over the future course of Reconstruction.

Opposite: Field workers sit outside a wooden shanty in Savannah, Georgia.

CONGRESS LOOKS SOUTH

On December 18, 1865, Congress returned from a nine-month recess. The Republican majority refused to admit the new representatives from the eleven former Confederate states. Instead, lawmakers began a lengthy debate over Reconstruction policy. Conservative Republicans generally approved of President Johnson's plan. Radicals wanted to completely overturn that plan and establish new Southern governments, which would be required to exclude former Confederates from power and grant black men the vote. Moderates proposed a middle course. While they believed that the freedpeople needed additional protections, they wanted to work with the president to modify his plan. They also did not believe that the South was ready for black suffrage.

President Andrew Johnson, in a photo taken by Mathew Brady. Johnson's administration was marked by bitter conflicts with Congress over Reconstruction policy.

To resolve their differences, congressional lawmakers formed a committee to investigate conditions in the South. The Joint Committee on Reconstruction called more than one hundred witnesses, including Southern whites, Southern blacks, and Freedmen's Bureau agents. Many of the witnesses described the rising tide of rebellion and violence sweeping the South. Their testimony convinced many moderate Republicans that decisive steps must be taken to protect the freedpeople and guarantee the loyalty of the new Southern governments.

In early 1866 Congress passed two Reconstruction measures. The Freedmen's Bureau Bill extended the life of the agency, which had originally been established for only one year. The Civil Rights Bill granted citizenship to all persons born in the United States, regardless of race. It guaranteed the right of African Americans to "full and equal benefit of all laws and proceedings for the security of person and property, as is enjoyed by white citizens." The bill also struck down the Southern laws that discriminated against blacks. Even though the Civil Rights Bill provided additional protections for the freedpeople, moderates believed that the president would support it because it did not include Radical provisions such as granting blacks the vote.

Instead, President Johnson vetoed both bills. In passionate speeches the president denounced Republicans who had supported the Freedmen's Bureau Bill as traitors to the Union. He argued that the Civil Rights Bill granted "the colored race safeguards which go infinitely beyond any that the General Government has ever provided for the white race." Johnson's actions united moderate and Radical Republicans against him. Congress overrode his vetoes to pass the bills. Then lawmakers went to work hammering out their own Reconstruction plan.

CONGRESSIONAL RECONSTRUCTION

The heart of the congressional Reconstruction plan was presented in two measures: the Fourteenth Amendment to the Constitution and the Reconstruction Acts.

The Fourteenth Amendment was intended to protect the freedpeople and prevent former Confederates from returning to power. Approved by Congress in June 1866, the amendment

SOUTHERN RACE RIOTS

Bloody race riots in American cities helped build support for Radical Reconstruction plans.

On May 1, 1866, a quarrel between white policemen and black army veterans in Memphis, Tennessee, exploded into a three-day race riot. Armed white gangs led by police and firefighters swarmed through the city, assaulting blacks and burning their homes, schools, and churches. At least forty-six African Americans were killed, and more than $130,000 worth of property was destroyed. A local white newspaper applauded the "lesson" taught by the Memphis riot: "The negroes now know, to their sorrow, that it is best not to arouse the fury of the white man."

Three months later, a second riot rocked New Orleans, Louisiana. African Americans and a group of armed white civilians and policemen had gathered outside a convention hall where delegates were meeting to discuss black enfranchisement. Words were exchanged, and shots rang out. Within minutes, the whites were shooting, stabbing, and beating the black men in the street and forcing their way inside the convention hall. By the time federal troops restored order, at least thirty-four blacks and three white delegates had been killed, and hundreds of others were wounded.

The massacres in Memphis and New Orleans helped convince Northern voters of the dangers of President Johnson's hands-off approach to Reconstruction. Candidates who opposed the president's policies won by a landslide in the congressional elections of 1866. With their huge majority in Congress, Republicans would have no trouble putting their plans for Reconstruction into action.

guaranteed basic legal and civil rights to all citizens, regardless of race, and disqualified former Confederate leaders from holding office. It also encouraged African-American suffrage by reducing congressional representation for states that did not give black men the vote. Congress demanded that Southern states ratify the Fourteenth Amendment before being readmitted to the Union. Every state refused except Tennessee, which approved the amendment and rejoined the Union in July 1866.

Beginning in March 1867, Congress passed four additional measures, known together as the Reconstruction Acts. This important legislation marked the beginning of the second stage of Reconstruction, often called Congressional or Radical Reconstruction. During this period, which would last until the end of Reconstruction in 1877, the Radical Republicans would play a major role in shaping Reconstruction policy.

The Reconstruction Acts dissolved the governments of the ten Southern states that had refused to ratify the Fourteenth Amendment. The South would be divided into five military districts, to be ruled by military commanders. The commanders would supervise the registration of black voters and the election of delegates to state constitutional conventions. Each state would draft a new constitution ratifying the Fourteenth Amendment and extending suffrage to all adult males "of whatever race, color, or previous condition." Once a state ratified its constitution, it could form a new government and rejoin the Union. Former Confederate leaders were barred from voting for convention delegates or voting on the new constitutions.

President Johnson denounced the Reconstruction Acts. It was "worse than madness," he declared, to give inexperienced black voters the power "to rule the white race." In the months

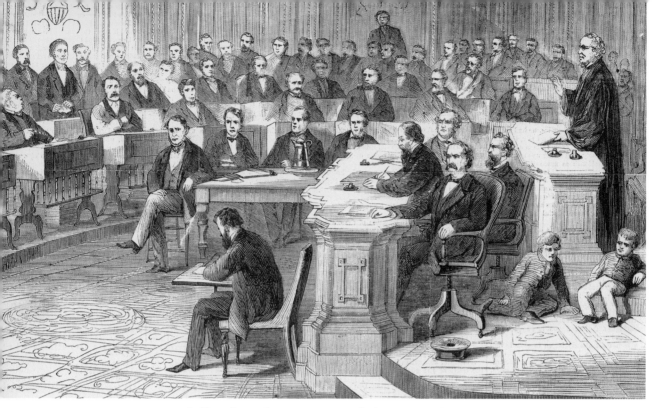

Senators vote in the impeachment trial of Andrew Johnson. They would come within a single vote of removing the president from office.

following the passage of the acts, the president did everything possible to interfere with Congressional Reconstruction. His actions further infuriated Radical Republicans and turned an ever-growing number of moderates against him.

Finally, the conflict reached a climax. In early 1868 the Radical Republicans launched a drive to impeach the president. On May 16 the Senate voted 35 to 19 to convict Johnson of "high crimes and misdemeanors"—one vote short of the two-thirds majority needed to remove him from office. President Johnson was cleared of all charges. The controversy had greatly weakened his power, however, and his term was coming to an end. In November the Republican candidate Ulysses S. Grant would replace Andrew Johnson as president.

FREEDMEN CAST THEIR BALLOTS
While Washington was consumed with the impeachment trial of Andrew Johnson, a political revolution was taking place in

the South. Under the terms of the Reconstruction Acts, the commanders of the Southern military districts began preparing for the state constitutional conventions. Eager to exercise their new rights as citizens, the vast majority of black men registered to vote. Many African Americans also took part in political rallies, parades, lectures, and debates. Thousands joined political organizations such as the Union League, a group linked to the Northern Republican Party. Members of these political groups met in black homes, schools, and churches to discuss strategies for helping the freedpeople gain equal rights and opportunities. The groups also helped register, educate, and protect black voters. One unhappy white plantation manager summed up the situation: "You never saw a people more excited on the subject of politics than are the Negroes of the South. They are perfectly wild."

By the fall of 1867, about 735,000 blacks and 635,000 whites had registered to vote in the ten former Confederate states. Fewer than half of the white voters turned out for the elections for convention delegates. Meanwhile, four-fifths of black voters proudly cast their first ballots. These new voters had overcome determined efforts by Southern whites to suppress or influence their votes. Bands of armed whites had menaced African Americans at voter registration sites. Other former Confederates pressured the freedmen to support the Democratic candidates. One Mississippi freedman reported that his employer vowed to "put a bullet through me if I voted the Republican ticket." Another was "met by a lot of white folks" at the polls. "The men gathered round and forced me to vote the Democratic ticket."

The efforts to control the black vote failed. The freedmen overwhelmingly voted for the party of Lincoln and emancipation.

About three-quarters of the 1,042 delegates who won election were Republicans. More than one-quarter were black.

During the winter of 1867–1868, constitutional conventions met throughout the South. For the first time ever, white and black Americans worked together to write the fundamental laws of their states. The constitutions they produced were among the most progressive in the nation. At a time when thousands of African Americans were still denied suffrage in the North, the Southern constitutions granted the vote to all men (but no women), regardless of race. The constitutions also removed property requirements for sitting on juries and holding office and provided for the establishment of public schools for both races.

Black voters cast their first ballots in the nation's capital, June 1867. A local newspaper reported that the historic election "proceeded with remarkable quietude and good order."

When the time came to ratify the new constitutions and elect state officials, many white Southerners boycotted the polls. Others used threats and violence to discourage African Americans from voting. Once again those efforts failed. According to a Northern observer, blacks flocked to the polls "in defiance of fatigue, hardship, hunger, and threats of employers." Few of the voters owned a pair of shoes, and scarcely one out of fifty wore an "unpatched garment." Still, the freedmen stood in line for hours, many braving a "pitiless storm." Their determination, wrote the reporter, came from "the hunger to have the same chances as the white men."

CARPETBAGGERS, SCALAWAGS, AND BLACKS

By June 1870, all of the Southern states had ratified the Fourteenth Amendment as well as the Fifteenth Amendment, which granted voting rights to all male citizens, regardless of race. Every state had approved its constitution and rejoined the Union. The new Reconstruction governments were overwhelmingly Republican. The leaders of those governments fell into three categories: "carpetbaggers," "scalawags," and African Americans.

The carpetbaggers were white Northerners who had settled in the South after the Civil War. Hostile white Southerners gave this group its name, portraying the migrants as lowly crooks who had come south to rob the state treasuries, carrying all their belongings in a cheap traveler's bag. In reality, many carpetbaggers were former Union officers, federal officials, teachers, or clergymen who had worked with the freedpeople during the war. Others were businessmen who had moved south to take advantage of postwar economic and political opportunities. The carpetbaggers were a powerful force in the Reconstruction governments. They made up about 30 percent of all officeholders, and many served as governors, U.S. congressmen, and in other high-ranking posts.

Even more numerous than the carpetbaggers were members of the group mockingly called "scalawags," after a small island in Scotland known for its stunted cattle. The scalawags were white Southerners who supported Reconstruction. They included poor farmers who had long resented the "slaveholding aristocracy," as well as planters, businessmen, and other former Confederates who believed that the best way to restore the South was to work with the party in power. Opponents denounced the scalawags as traitors to their race who, as one angry Democrat put it, had "dishonored the dignity of white blood."

Black men held about 15 to 20 percent of the offices in Reconstruction governments. There were African Americans at every level, from city councils to the U.S. Congress. However, blacks were more numerous in local and state governments than in the national government. There were also more black officeholders in the Deep South, where the majority of slaves had lived at the start of the Civil War, than in the Upper South. African Americans served in important state posts including lieutenant governor, secretary of state, state treasurer, and superintendent of education, although none was elected governor. Nearly eight hundred African Americans served in state legislatures, but blacks held a majority in only one state, South Carolina. Two African Americans were elected to the U.S. Senate and fourteen to the House of Representatives.

African-American political leaders came from a broad range of backgrounds. They included clergymen, carpenters, blacksmiths, teachers, farmers, and field hands. While some black politicians had been born and raised in the North, most were native Southerners. They generally had more education than the mass of freedpeople. Many had been born free or had escaped to freedom before the war. The group also included many former slaves who had established their leadership in the black community as teachers, preachers, skilled craftsmen, or soldiers.

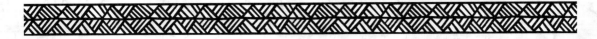

FROM SLAVERY TO THE STATE HOUSE

The majority of black Reconstruction officials were former slaves. Here are a few of the hundreds of freedmen whose talents, drive, and dedication led to successful political careers:

EMANUEL FORTUNE served five terms in the Florida state legislature. This former slave was described as a natural leader who had "commanded his time as a tanner and expert shoe and bootmaker. In such life as the slaves were allowed and in church work, he took the leader's part."

Georgia state legislator THOMAS ALLEN was a preacher, shoemaker, and farmer who had earned respect in the black community through his literacy. "In my county the colored people came to me for instructions," he explained. "I took the New York Tribune and other papers, and . . . I found out a great deal, and I told them whatever I thought was right."

The South Carolina legislature in 1873

JOHN R. LYNCH of Mississippi gained his freedom at age sixteen, when Union soldiers occupied his home state. The self-educated young man became active in a political club, where his passion and intelligence catapulted him into office. Lynch was elected to the Mississippi state legislature and then the U.S. House of Representatives. Despite his rise to high office, he was subjected to the same discrimination as all African Americans. During his official trips to Washington, Lynch reported, he was forced to sit in the "filthy smoking-car" reserved for blacks and treated "not as an American citizen, but as a brute."

BLANCHE K. BRUCE was a former slave from Virginia who had escaped to freedom in the early days of the Civil War. In 1869 he went to Mississippi with seventy-five cents in his pocket and forged a successful career as a sheriff, tax collector, and newspaper editor. Bruce was elected to the U.S. Senate in 1874. He became an outspoken defender of the civil rights of African Americans as well as Native Americans and Chinese immigrants.

RECONSTRUCTION SUCCESSES AND FAILURES

The leaders of the Reconstruction governments were responsible for many advances. Their greatest achievement was the establishment of the first statewide public school systems in the South. Before the war, education was largely limited to white children from wealthy families. By 1876, more than half of the South's white children and two-fifths of black children were enrolled in public schools.

Reconstruction governments also established aid for the poor, disabled, mentally ill, and orphans. Several states repealed the Black Codes, reformed their tax systems, and reorganized and modernized judicial systems and prisons. To promote economic recovery, Republican lawmakers supported railroad construction and rebuilt roads, dams, bridges, and other structures that had been damaged during the war.

Some Southern states also passed legislation banning discrimination in public transportation and public buildings. In Louisiana, Mississippi, South Carolina, Florida, and Arkansas, it became illegal for streetcars, railroads, steamboats, hotels, and other institutions to segregate or exclude blacks. These antidiscrimination laws were not always enforced. However, they marked the first time that any state, North or South, had recognized the right of African Americans to equality in public services. In 1873 a Northern reporter could hardly believe "that the many Negroes one sees . . . [had] been slaves a few short years ago, at least as far as their demeanor [behavior] goes as individuals newly invested with all the rights and privileges of an American citizen."

Along with the many achievements of the Reconstruction governments came some notable disappointments. Southern white opposition and divisions within their own party prevented Republican lawmakers from reaching a number of their goals. Their efforts to promote economic development in the South were not very successful. Their new public schools were almost completely segregated. In fact, racial separation and discrimination remained widespread throughout the South. Most significant of all, the Reconstruction governments did almost nothing to help the freedpeople acquire land. As a result, most Southern blacks remained locked in poverty as laborers on white-owned farms and plantations.

Although the number of African-American officeholders increased slightly as blacks gained political experience, they never served in numbers representative of their population in the South. Nevertheless, black political leaders had a tremendous impact on the Reconstruction governments. At the local level, African-American officials helped make sure that blacks received their fair share of government services such as road repair and aid to the poor. Black police chiefs, judges, and justices of the peace ensured that the freedpeople received equal treatment under the law. The image of African Americans helping to govern states that had until recently held them in bondage was also a dramatic sign of the many changes sweeping the South.

White supremacists wearing ghostly masks and sheets terrorize a Southern black family.

Chapter 6

Retreat from Reconstruction

THE GREAT MAJORITY OF WHITE SOUTHERNERS bitterly opposed Reconstruction. They resented Northern interference in their affairs and the continued presence of federal troops in the South. Most of all, they could not bear the sight of former slaves voting, holding office, and demanding equal treatment under the law. From the moment Southern Republicans rose to power, Democrats cried out against the "Africanization" of state governments, charging that whites were being "trodden under foot by an inferior and barbarous race." After the election of Ulysses S. Grant in 1868, Reconstruction opponents became increasingly united in their efforts to restore white supremacy throughout the South. Their methods included fraud, intimidation, and a campaign of violence that reduced the freedpeople to what one Alabama sharecropper called "such a state of fear that life itself is almost insupportable."

A Reign of Terror

In 1868 Benjamin Randolph, an African-American state senator from South Carolina, was shot and killed by white assassins. Abram Colby, who had been elected to the Georgia state legislature, was beaten by white assailants as his "little daughter begged them not to carry me away." George Moore of Alabama reported that he had been beaten by whites who also wounded his neighbor and "ravished a young girl who was visiting my wife. . . . The cause of this treatment, they said, was that we voted the radical ticket."

The freedpeople had endured random acts of violence ever since the Civil War's end. By 1868, however, the attacks were becoming more widespread and better organized. The enemies of Reconstruction had a new mission. Instead of simply punishing individual freedmen for asserting their rights, white terrorists planned to use threats and violence as tools for the destruction of Republican rule.

The terrorist organizations went by different names in different states, including the Knights of the White Camellia in Louisiana and the Knights of the Rising Sun in Texas. The most prominent group, however, was the "Invisible Empire of the South," commonly known as the Ku Klux Klan. The Klan was founded around 1866 by Confederate veterans in Tennessee. It quickly grew into a massive organization with half a million members and branches in nearly every Southern state. Members of this secret order came from all walks of life, including lawyers, judges, clergymen, plantation owners, and poor white farmers. Their targets were Republican leaders and voters, both black and white, as well as freedpeople who complained about their wages, left their employers, bought land, learned to read and write, or in any other way challenged white supremacy. Under cover of darkness, groups of Klansmen wearing ghostly white robes and hoods whipped, tortured, raped, shot, or hanged their victims. The Klan "night riders" also burned black homes, schools, and churches.

In 1871 Robert Gleed, a former slave and Mississippi state senator, testified before a U.S. congressional committee investigating the Ku Klux Klan. Describing racial violence in his state as a "reign of terror," Gleed reported that the Klan's purpose was "to remand [return] the colored men of the country to as near a position of servitude as possible, and to destroy the republican party if possible; . . . We believe it had two objects, one was political, and the other was to hold the black man in subjection to the white man, and to have white supremacy in the South."

A "night rider" of the Ku Klux Klan, the most prominent terrorist organization of the Reconstruction era

According to some estimates, the Ku Klux Klan killed about twenty thousand men, women, and children between 1868 and 1871 and brutally attacked tens of thousands more. Countless Republican leaders were driven from their homes and offices. Countless black men were prevented from voting. By 1871, the Republican Party in many areas of the South had been, in the words of one observer, "scattered and beaten and run out."

FIGHTING BACK

Southern blacks did not submit quietly to Klan rule. Men who owned guns tried to defend their families and guard the homes of their teachers and political leaders. In some areas African Americans organized militias and other military groups. The black citizens of Bennettsville, South Carolina, put an end to Klan assaults through armed street patrols. In Blount County, Alabama, white Union veterans who grew sick of the violence formed their own "anti-Ku Klux." The group restored the peace by threatening to kill Klansmen unless they stopped attacking Republican office-holders and burning black schools and churches.

But the Klan and other white terrorist groups were too large, well organized, and well armed to be stopped by citizens alone. Even local and state governments often proved ineffective or powerless. In many Southern communities, white sheriffs and policemen sympathized with the Klan or lacked the courage to oppose it. In the rare cases where Klansmen were arrested and tried for their crimes, witnesses often refused to testify against them, either because they were afraid or because they supported Klan activities. On the state level, governors were reluctant to call out their mostly black militias, for fear of triggering race riots.

Between 1870 and 1871, Congress took matters into its own hands, passing a series of laws known as the Enforcement Acts. These criminal codes defended the right of African Americans to vote, hold office, serve on juries, and receive equal treatment under the law. Any criminal act aimed at depriving a citizen of those rights became a federal offense. That gave the president the authority to send in federal troops to restore law and order.

In 1871 President Grant ordered federal marshals, backed up by the army, to arrest thousands of accused Klansmen across the

South. Hundreds of white terrorists were tried and convicted in federal courts. By 1872, the Ku Klux Klan was out of business and peace was restored in the South, at least temporarily.

President Ulysses S. Grant signs the Ku Klux Klan Act of 1871, which authorized the federal government to act against terrorist organizations.

BEGINNING OF THE END

The Klan's reign of terror had greatly weakened the Republican Party in the South. Reconstruction leaders also faced other serious challenges. Claims of widespread corruption were eroding support for the Southern state governments. The high taxes needed to fund Reconstruction programs were driving white property owners into the Democratic camp. Meanwhile, continuing conflicts within the Republican Party were unraveling the fragile partnership of black officeholders, carpetbaggers, and scalawags.

Under pressure from fellow white Southerners, scalawags had begun to abandon the Republican Party as early as 1869. In some states Democrats joined with the dissenting Republicans to regain control of the governments. This process, which the Democrats called "redeeming" the Southern governments, put an end to Reconstruction in those states. Virginia and Tennessee were "redeemed" in 1869, North Carolina in 1870, and Georgia in 1871.

In 1872 a large number of prominent scalawags deserted the Republican Party, denouncing widespread corruption in the Grant administration. Calling themselves the Liberal Republicans, this group supported Democratic candidate Horace Greeley against Grant in that year's presidential race. Despite their opposition, President Grant won reelection. For Republicans, though, the victory was bittersweet. They had held on to power, but they had lost the support of the majority of white Southerners.

Following the presidential election, the Democrats and Liberal Republicans continued their attacks on the Reconstruction governments. The South's problems, they maintained, were the result of misgovernment by crooked, incompetent former slaves and carpetbaggers. Only through a return to "home rule" by the "best men" of the South could the states root out corruption and ensure a lasting peace.

More and more Northerners began to accept those arguments. In 1873 the nation entered a severe economic depression, with widespread business failures and high unemployment. Concerned about their own futures, Northerners grew increasingly weary of the costs of Reconstruction. They were also discouraged by the constant reports of turmoil in the South. Even Radical Republicans began to doubt that the troubled Reconstruction governments would ever solve the region's deep and persistent problems. People were tired of "the negro question with all its complications," reported a leading Republican newspaper, "and the reconstruction of the southern States, with all its interminable embroilments."

Terror in Mississippi

As national support for Reconstruction declined, Southern governments continued to topple. The Democrats regained control of Texas in 1873 and Arkansas and Alabama in 1874. In the states where Reconstruction endured, opponents unleashed a new wave of violence. New terrorist groups formed, including the White League in Louisiana, the Rifle Clubs in Mississippi, and the Red Shirts in South Carolina. Unlike the night riders of the Ku Klux Klan, the defiant members of these organizations committed their crimes in broad daylight. They burned government buildings, assaulted Republican officials, and terrorized black voters.

"It was the most violent time that ever we have seen," recalled former state senator Robert Gleed of Mississippi. The Rifle Clubs set fire to Gleed's home and hundreds of other buildings owned by black and white Republicans during the state's 1875 election season. Organized in cavalry units, armed terrorists rode through the countryside, threatening to kill any black man who tried to vote. They openly assaulted and murdered Republican leaders. They provoked fights that quickly escalated into shooting sprees. In Clinton, Mississippi, a group of white men opened fire on a Republican rally, then "hunted the whole county clean out," shooting black men "just the same as

The White League seizes the Louisiana State House in New Orleans, September 1874. Federal troops had to be called in to restore the state's Republican government.

birds." A similar rampage in Vicksburg left at least thirty-five freedmen dead. When Mississippi governor Adelbert Ames appealed to the federal government for help, President Grant refused to send troops, noting that the "whole public are tired out with these annual autumnal outbreaks in the South."

On election day white men armed with rifles and cannons watched over Mississippi polling places. Freedmen who defied the guards were turned away by Democratic election officials, who claimed that their names were not in the books of registered voters. After the polls closed, the same officials destroyed Republican ballots and substituted their own. Not surprisingly, the Democrats overwhelmingly carried the election, ending Reconstruction in Mississippi.

THE COMPROMISE OF 1877

In 1876 Republican candidate Rutherford B. Hayes faced Democrat Samuel J. Tilden for the presidency. Elections for state offices were also being held in the three remaining Southern states with Republican governments: Louisiana, South Carolina, and Florida. Once again armed whites used intimidation, violence, and fraud in support of the anti-Reconstruction candidates. This time, however, the election results were so close that both the Republicans and Democrats claimed victories. In Louisiana and South Carolina, both parties organized their own independent legislatures and installed their own governors. The disputed results also left the nation with an even more serious dilemma. The contest between Hayes and Tilden was so close that whoever won the three "unredeemed" Southern states would become president.

To resolve the crisis, Congress appointed a special electoral

W. E. B. DuBOIS REWRITES RECONSTRUCTION

For many years historians viewed Reconstruction as a colossal failure. According to their accounts, Southern Republican leaders were incompetent and corrupt, and Southern whites were justified in overthrowing their governments. In the early 1900s, African-American activist and scholar W. E. B. DuBois challenged that view. In his book *Black Reconstruction in America,* DuBois portrayed Reconstruction as a "brave and fine fight" to build a truly democratic society on the ashes of slavery. While he acknowledged that there were unscrupulous Reconstruction politicians, DuBois pointed out that government corruption was widespread in the post–Civil War era, in both North and South, among both Republicans and Democrats. He also argued that many African-American leaders were exceptionally honest, industrious, and effective. Finally, DuBois maintained that Reconstruction was a time of important advances in the education and economic and political standing of the former slaves. While the "attempt to make black men American citizens was in a certain sense all a failure," he wrote, it was "a splendid failure." W. E. B. DuBois' writings forced scholars to rethink their ideas on Reconstruction, leading to a radically new view of one of the most controversial periods in American history.

Above: W. E. B. DuBois was a writer, editor, educator, activist, and a cofounder of the NAACP (National Association for the Advancement of Colored People).

commission made up of both Democrats and Republicans. The commission worked out a compromise that gave the presidency to Hayes. In return, the Republicans promised the Democrats that the new president would end federal intervention in the South. In March 1877 Rutherford B. Hayes was sworn in as president. As one of his first acts, he withdrew the federal troops from Southern capitals. Without federal protection, the Republican governments quickly collapsed. The Democrats now ruled the entire South. Reconstruction was at an end.

The new Southern Democratic governments would soon roll back the advances of Reconstruction. New laws and practices would deny black voting rights and provide for the strict segregation of the races. Labor laws would empower white employers and condemn black laborers to decades of exploitation and poverty. Violence against African Americans who strove to improve their situation would become a part of Southern life. Twenty-five years after the end of Reconstruction, civil rights activist and scholar W. E. B. DuBois would declare, "Despite compromise, war, and struggle the Negro is not free."

At the same time, Reconstruction had laid the foundation for the important changes that would take place during the Civil Rights movement nearly a century later. The Fourteenth and Fifteenth Amendments would provide the legal basis for that era's advances in civil and political rights. Reconstruction had also given rise to a vast network of black schools and churches. These institutions would help sustain African-American society through the continuing struggle for equality, justice, and full citizenship.

Glossary

abolition The act of abolishing, or putting an end to, slavery.

amnesty A formal pardon granted to a group of people, releasing them from punishment for their offenses.

Black Codes Laws passed by state and local governments in the South during Reconstruction to restrict the rights and freedoms of former slaves.

border states The slaveholding states on the border between the North and South, which included Delaware, Kentucky, Maryland, Missouri, and Virginia. Only Virginia joined the Confederacy.

carpetbaggers The insulting name given by hostile white Southerners to white Northern Republicans who settled in the South after the Civil War and held office in the Reconstruction governments.

Confederate Belonging to the Southern states that seceded from the Union during the Civil War, forming a new republic, the Confederate States of America. The Confederate states were Alabama, Arkansas, Florida, Georgia, Louisiana, Mississippi, North Carolina, South Carolina, Tennessee, Texas, and Virginia.

Deep South The southeastern states (usually considered to include Alabama, Georgia, Louisiana, and parts of Mississippi, Arkansas, and Texas) where most slaves lived at the start of the Civil War.

emancipation Freeing someone from the control or power of another.

enfranchisement The act of granting someone the rights of citizenship, especially the right to vote.

impeach To charge a public official with crimes, in order to remove the official from office.

overseers Men who were hired to supervise the slave laborers on Southern plantations.

refugees People who flee from an area to escape hardship or danger.

secession The act of seceding, or formally withdrawing from a group.

segregation The practice of keeping one race apart from another by setting up separate housing, schools, and public facilities and through other forms of discrimination.

suffrage The right to vote.

Upper South The Southern slaveholding states of Delaware, Kentucky, Maryland, Missouri, North Carolina, Tennessee, and Virginia, plus Washington, DC.

vagrancy The state of being a vagrant, a person without a home or regular work.

To Find Out More

BOOKS

Dudley, William, ed. *Reconstruction.* San Diego, CA: Greenhaven Press, 2003.

Flanagan, Timothy. *Reconstruction: A Primary Source History of the Struggle to Unite the North and South after the Civil War.* New York: Rosen, 2005.

Greene, Meg. *Into the Land of Freedom: African Americans in Reconstruction.* Minneapolis, MN: Lerner, 2004.

Hansen, Joyce. *"Bury Me Not in a Land of Slaves": African-Americans in the Time of Reconstruction.* New York: Franklin Watts, 2000.

Mettger, Zak. *Reconstruction: America after the Civil War.* New York: Lodestar Books, 1994.

Ruggiero, Adriane. *American Voices from Reconstruction.* New York: Benchmark Books, 2006.

Smith, John David. *Black Voices from Reconstruction, 1865–1877.* Brookfield, CT: Millbrook Press, 1996.

Stefoff, Rebecca. *The Civil War and Reconstruction, 1863–1877.* New York: Benchmark Books, 2003.

Ziff, Marsha. *Reconstruction following the Civil War in American History.* Berkeley Heights, NJ: Enslow Publishers, 1999.

WEB SITES

African American Odyssey: Reconstruction and Its Aftermath. Library of Congress.
http://memory.loc.gov/ammem/aaohtml/exhibit/aopart5.html

America's Reconstruction: People and Politics after the Civil War. Copyright 2004 Digital History, University of Houston.
www.digitalhistory.uh.edu/reconstruction/index.html

Jump Back in Time: Reconstruction (1866–1877). Library of Congress.
www.americaslibrary.gov/cgi-bin/page.cgi/jb/recon

Reconstruction. Spartacus Educational.
www.spartacus.schoolnet.co.uk/USASreconstruction.htm

Reconstruction: The Second Civil War. Copyright 1997–2004 PBS Online/WGBH.
www.pbs.org/wgbh/amex/reconstruction

Bibliography

Blight, David W. *Race and Reunion: The Civil War in American Memory.* Cambridge, MA: Harvard University Press, 2001.

DuBois, W. E. B. *Black Reconstruction in America, 1860–1880.* New York: Free Press, 1998.

Foner, Eric. *Reconstruction: America's Unfinished Revolution, 1863–1877.* New York: Harper & Row, 1988.

Foner, Eric, and Olivia Mahoney. *America's Reconstruction: People and Politics after the Civil War.* New York: HarperCollins, 1995.

Franklin, John Hope, and Alfred A. Moss Jr. *From Slavery to Freedom: A History of African Americans.* New York: Alfred A. Knopf, 2004.

Horton, James Oliver, and Lois E. Horton. *Slavery and the Making of America.* New York: Oxford University Press, 2005.

Litwack, Leon F. *Been in the Storm So Long: The Aftermath of Slavery.* New York: Vintage Books, 1980.

McPherson, James M. *Ordeal by Fire: The Civil War and Reconstruction.* New York: McGraw-Hill, 2001.

Perman, Michael. *Emancipation and Reconstruction.* Wheeling, IL: Harlan Davidson, 2003.

Rabinowitz, Howard N., ed. *Southern Black Leaders of the Reconstruction Era.* Urbana, IL: University of Illinois Press, 1982.

Sterling, Dorothy, ed. *The Trouble They Seen: The Story of Reconstruction in the Words of African Americans.* New York: Da Capo, 1994.

Trefousse, Hans L. *Historical Dictionary of Reconstruction.* New York: Greenwood Press, 1991.

Trowbridge, J. T. *The South: A Tour of Its Battle-fields and Ruined Cities.* Hartford, CT: L. Stebbins, 1866; reprint, New York: Arno Press, 1969.

Index

Page numbers for illustrations are in boldface